LET'S GET STARTED!

Exercise your brain with these challenging puzzles!

From unscrambling numbers, mental arithmetic, and memory games to mazes, word searches, and spot the difference puzzles, this book has it all. Look for patterns in picture, number, and letter sequences—it may help to read them aloud or write them in a line. If you are confused by a puzzle, leave it to one side and come back to it later. You can use the answers at the back if you're totally stuck.

Have fun!

Treasure trove

Use the clues to figure out who did what on their day at the beach, and who they were there with. Each person did just **one** activity, and each person did a **different** activity, and was with a **different** group.

Jacob and Mimi went in the water.

Bo was with her family. She didn't build a sandcastle.

The person who swam was with school.

Mimi was with the Scouts.

	Jacob	Mimi	Abe	Bo
Sandcastle				
Swim				
Paddleboard				
Sunbathe				
Family				
School				
Scouts				
Friends				

4

TRAIN YOUR BRAIN!
BRAIN TEASERS

ARCTURUS

This edition published in 2024 by Arcturus Publishing Limited
26/27 Bickels Yard, 151–153 Bermondsey Street,
London SE1 3HA

Author: Lisa Regan
Illustrator: Evelyn Rogers
Editor: Lydia Halliday
Designer: Amy McSimpson
Managing Editor: Joe Harris
Managing Designer: Georgina Wood

ISBN: 978-1-3988-3110-0
CH010837NT
Supplier 29, Date 0124, PI 00004144

Printed in China

Big city lights

Which of the tiles underneath does not appear in this city skyline?

Now use your eagle eyes to answer these questions:

Which are there more of, buildings with orange lights or buildings with blue lights?

How many buildings are taller than the rainbow building?

How many buildings have a triangular roof?

Move it!

The limos are blocking the other cars, so the parking attendant wants to move them into their own area. By taking a limousine and directly swapping it with an ordinary car, what's the smallest number of moves it would take to have only one sort of vehicle parked in each section? Each swap counts as two moves.

Chilling out

Find all the letters that have an odd number next to them. Put them in the right order, and they will spell out a type of penguin that can be found in a number of countries in the southern hemisphere.

All the balls

Without taking your pencil off the page, can you draw a route that connects all nine balls, but uses just four straight lines? The coaches each have a hint, if you're feeling baffled.

Hint 1: Start at the tennis ball in the bottom right corner.

Hint 2: Your line can extend farther than the balls.

Found in the forest

Take a look at this image of a lively rain forest.
Then turn the page to see how much you remember.

Look really closely
to see if you can spot
each of these.

Found in the forest

Answer the questions below to see what you can remember from the scene without turning back.

1. How many tapirs were snuffling on the forest floor?
2. What two creatures were in the sky above the trees?
3. Which were there more of, blue macaws or scarlet macaws?
4. Where was the jaguar?
5. Nearly all the frogs had black markings. Which was the only one without?
6. How many green tree snakes did you spot?
7. Which was bigger, the green butterfly or the blue one?
8. What creature was lurking by the red flower on the forest floor?
9. How many types of monkey did you see?
10. Which creature was the highest in the tree canopy?

Now find the names of these rainforest animals, hiding away in the grid.

TAPIR
JAGUAR
TOUCAN
SLOTH
MACAW
ANACONDA
ANTEATER
CAPYBARA

A	E	F	W	A	E	J	A	G	U	A	R	J	E	D
M	Y	J	D	Z	N	I	R	B	K	Y	W	U	U	L
I	T	O	F	H	C	T	F	I	X	A	T	A	S	V
E	O	S	C	G	B	A	E	W	C	J	M	N	N	I
T	U	T	V	T	U	R	U	A	Q	Z	O	A	E	T
B	C	H	J	S	W	E	M	L	T	I	N	C	U	Q
C	A	P	Y	B	A	R	A	S	A	E	Y	O	B	A
A	N	I	K	X	J	Y	M	K	P	U	R	N	V	W
T	O	Y	S	L	O	T	H	L	I	M	E	D	U	N
I	W	Q	U	J	K	X	N	O	R	B	Y	A	I	J

Picnic puzzler

Draw a line to connect each picnic item with another item of the same type. The lines can go up, down, and across, but not diagonally. Only one line should pass through each blanket square. Crossing over another line isn't allowed. One line has been drawn to start you off.

Who goes there?

The names of three mythical creatures are hidden in these letters. Can you find them? Circle all of the leftover letters to find out what feature they all have in common.

WSPHINXIGRIFFINNPEGASUSGS

Do you know which is which? Label each one underneath its picture.

1. _____

2. _____

3. _____

All wrapped up

What has been beautifully gift wrapped in each of these presents? Use the code to work it out. To get started, fill in the grid: the first present is a BRACELET.

23.14.19.12

7.23.6.8.10.17.10.25

19.10.8.16.17.6.8.10

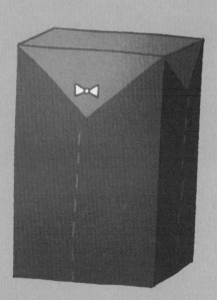

25.14.6.23.6

A	B	C	D	E	F	G	H	I	J	K	L	M	N	O	P	Q	R	S	T	U	V	W	X	Y	Z

An eggs-act amount

There are three farmers, and each has a different number of new ducklings on their farm. One of them has 2, one of them has 4, and one of them has 8.

Using the clues below, can you work out which farmer lives on each farm, and how many ducklings each has?

The farmer that lives on Blossom Farm has fewer ducklings than Farmer Ben.

Farmer Tom has twice as many ducklings as Farmer Frieda.

Farmer Frieda does not live on Blossom Farm or Manor Farm.

The farmer who lives on Blossom Farm has more ducklings than the farmer who lives on Hall Farm.

Farmer	Farm	Number of ducklings

Flying high

All of these dragonflies look identical, apart from one. Can you spot it?

On safari

Help the guide lead the tourists to the viewing hut by following the compass directions. N3 means go north 3 squares, E4 means go east 4 squares, and so on. Which set of directions gives them a clear path to reach the "X"? Start at the bottom right square.

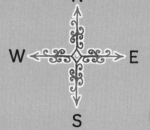

Do you drive W5, N3, E1, N2, W1, N2, W3, N1, E5?   Or W5, N3, E1, N2, W1, N1, W2, N2, E3?

Or W3, N1, W4, N3, W2, N6, E5, S2, E2?   Or N2, W4, N4, E3, N1?

Hop along

These bunnies were having a race. Using the clues below, can you work out in which order they finished?

The brown bunny finished two places behind the biggest bunny.

The spotted bunny was ahead of three others.

The white bunny didn't finish last.

The biggest bunny was ahead of the spotted bunny.

Bunny	Place

Blue planet

Use the letters of the alphabet that are missing from each shell to find the names of four different creatures that are found in the ocean.

A
DEFG
MNOP YZ
QSTUV
WX
HIJKL

B
GIJ KMN
OPQRS TUVX
YZ BCDF

C
NO BCD M
G YZ
PQT
WX
EF UV IJL

D
AB MNO
PR GH TV
WX JKL
CEF YZ

Fairy finds

Can you help Pixie Flyn find these groups of flowers in the grid below? Each group appears just once.

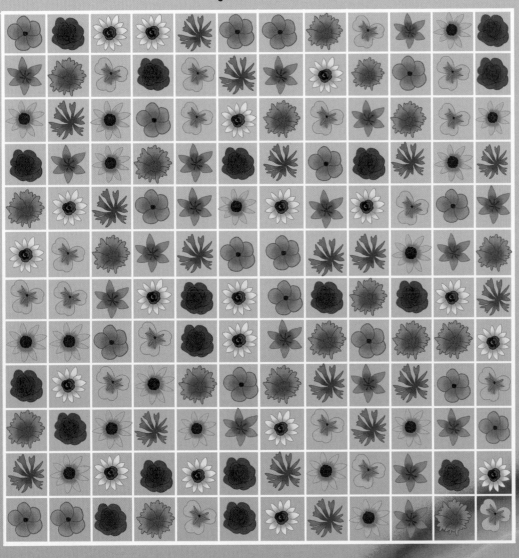

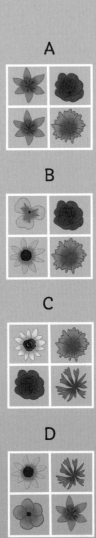

A

B

C

D

Gone missing

If each meerkat has five pups, how many pups are missing from this picture?
Don't worry—they'll turn up soon!

A witch's brew

Which potion does the witch need to conjure up to complete the sequence? Is it potion A, B, C, or D?

A

B

C

D

Madame Marrow uses ten mixing jars for her three potions. The red potion uses two mixing jars. The green and purple potions use more jars, but each uses the same number. How many jars does she use for the green potion?

Lost and found

This map tells forgetful Mother Hen where she has laid her eggs. Can you draw them onto the grid? Each number shows how many eggs are in the blank squares touching that square—up and down, across, or diagonally. There can only be one egg in each square.

Dressing up

Do you love pretending to be someone else, and trying on different clothes? See how many new words, with three letters or more, you can make from the phrase below.

COSTUME
PARTY

All change

Some of these chameleons are big, but others are small. Can you work out their order from biggest to smallest? Write out your answers on the leaves below. The first one has been done for you to get you started.

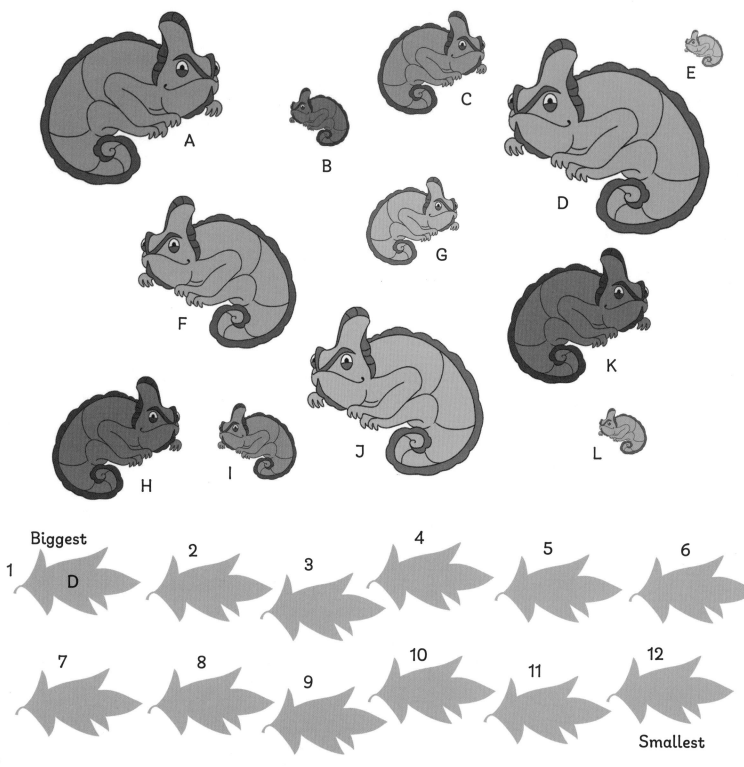

Biggest

1 D
2
3
4
5
6
7
8
9
10
11
12

Smallest

Play time

Three friends visited the same play area on different days. Each went on one piece of equipment. The weather was different on each day. Can you work out who played on what, and what the weather was like when they visited?

Serge didn't go on the slide as it was too wet from the rain.

Caitlin stayed home when it was windy. She played on the swings.

Name	Equipment	Weather

Anna wasn't there on a sunny day. She doesn't like the climbing frame.

Cruise control

Connect the islands with straight lines. The number of lines connected to each island must match the number written on that island. Each line must travel either horizontally (left to right) or vertically (up and down). The lines can't cross any other lines or islands. No more than two paths connect any pair of islands. Some lines are already in place.

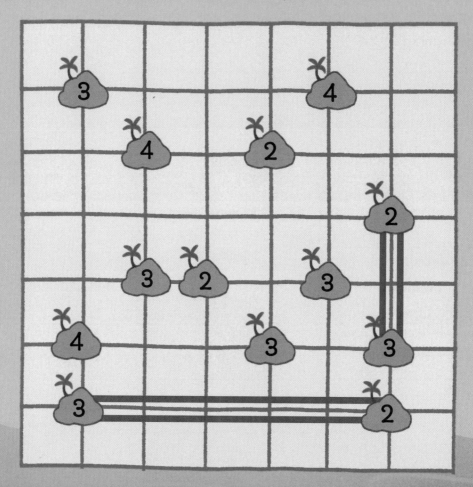

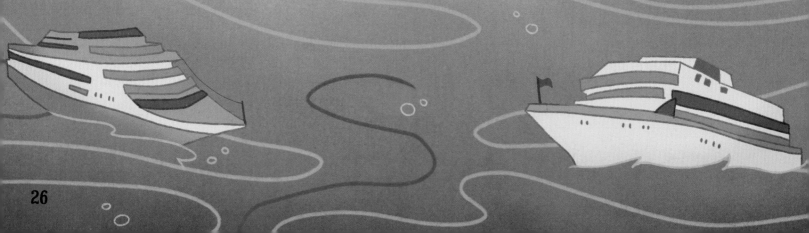

Lucky numbers

Nico's lucky number is nine. Draw shapes around the squares to join them into groups. The numbers in each group must add up to exactly nine. Every square must be in a group, and a square may not be in more than one group. The numbers in a group must touch on the sides, top, or bottom. Each group can be made up of any number of squares from two to five. The first one has been done for you. There are two puzzles to try!

Sand art

This sandcastle has been decorated with shells. Can you find the names of two shells CONCH and COWRIE hidden in the letter grid? Each name can be found twice, either across, up, down, or diagonally.

C	O	N	C	C	O	W	R	O	C
O	E	C	O	N	O	C	O	W	O
N	I	O	W	R	I	W	I	R	W
O	R	C	R	C	O	N	R	O	C
N	C	O	C	O	N	C	H	I	O
C	O	W	H	H	C	O	R	I	E
H	W	O	C	O	N	H	C	O	W
N	R	N	C	O	W	R	I	E	E
O	O	C	O	W	C	H	N	O	I
C	O	N	N	C	O	W	R	I	R

Metamorphosis

Only one butterfly can feed from a single flower. If each caterpillar changes into a butterfly, then joins the other butterflies in the park, will there be enough flowers in bloom to feed all the butterflies?

Magic convention

Can you find each of these wizard hats somewhere in the crowd?

Fast food

Superstack Burgers are doing big business today, and they're selling out fast. They don't have enough ingredients to make their full super-stack for all their remaining 80 burgers. If these are the percentages, what number of burgers get each of the toppings?

Only 15% of the burgers will get mushrooms.

25% of the burgers can have onions.

40% of the burgers will get cheese.

There's enough pickle for 55% of the burgers.

75% of the burgers can have tomato.

Toppings	Number of burgers

Flying high

Help the in-flight attendant work out if she can make all of her connections and be back in time for her aunt's birthday party at 7pm.

She leaves her hotel at 7am and needs an hour to get to the airport.

Her first flight takes off at 8:30am.

It's a 4-hour flight to a country that is in a time zone an hour ahead.

She takes 45 minutes for lunch before boarding her next flight.

That flight is scheduled to take off at 2:30pm.

It's a three-hour flight and it takes off and lands on time.

She allows an hour to get through the airport and grab a taxi. It's a 30-minute taxi ride to her aunt's home.

Will she make it?

Walking on the Moon

How many astronaut footprints can you count here? Can you spot four footprints that are walking in the opposite direction from the others?

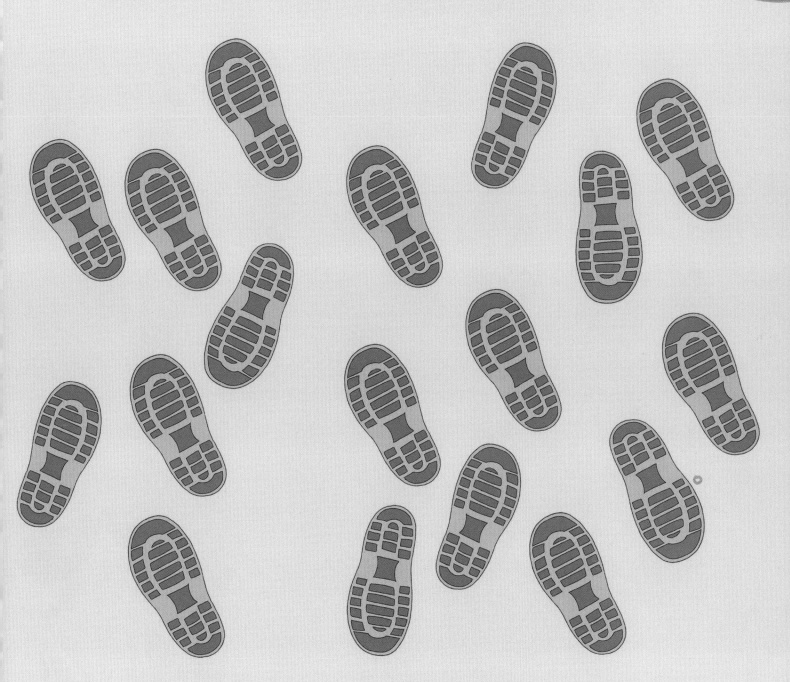

When did people first walk on the Moon?
Do the mathematics to work it out, working from left to right.

$$(111 \times 5) \times 2 \div 0.5 - 251$$

Pattern placement

Help the dressmaker pin her patterns onto the fabric correctly. Each L-shaped piece should contain just one of each of the four pictures. Use the whole fabric, with no scraps left over.

Odd one out

All of these ducks look identical, apart from one. Can you spot it?

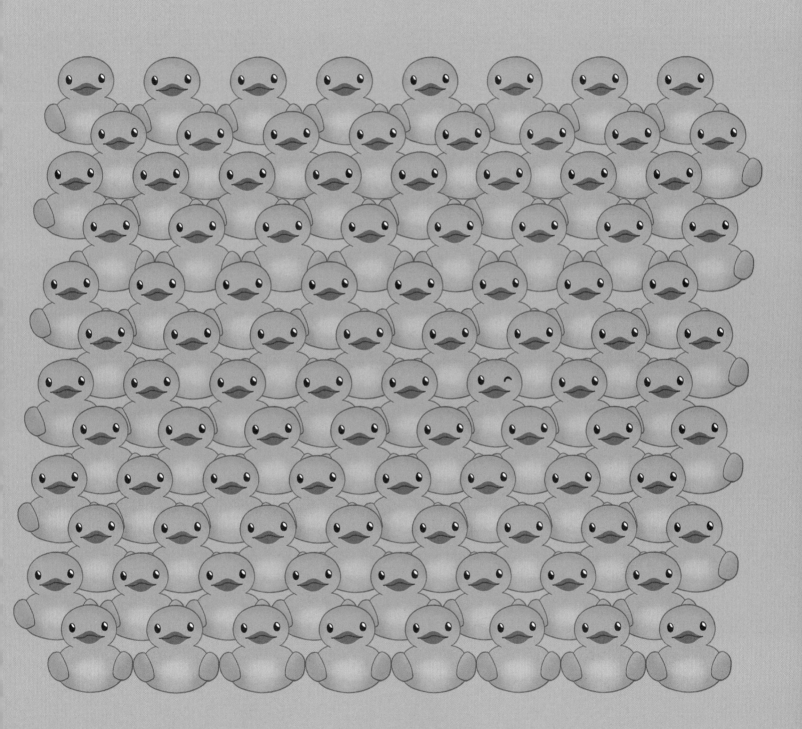

Cacti count

How many of each type of cactus can you count on this desert landscape?

Cross out every other letter around this cactus, starting with the X and working clockwise. The remaining letters spell the name of a US desert that is famous for its cacti.

Hard work

Which of these groups of letters is the only one that cannot be rearranged to spell AARDVARK?

RAARDKVA

VAKARDKR

VAKARDAR

ARARDVAK

DRAKARAV

KRAVARDA

KAVARDAR

Give me an "A"

While we're looking at spellings, see how you fare with these. All of the vowels have been taken out of the descriptions of these people. Can you work out what they should say?

Neil Armstrong FRST MN N TH MN

George Washington FRST PRSDNT F TH NTD STTS

Marie Curie FRST FML WNNR F TH NBL PRZ

Steve Jobs C-FNDR F TH PPL CMPNY

Albert Einstein DVLPD TH THRY F RLTVTY

Leonardo da Vinci PNTD TH MN LS

Serena Williams N F TH GRTST TNNS PLYRS

Dwayne Johnson GRT CTR KNWN S TH RCK

Jane Austen GRT NGLSH NVLST

Martin Luther King LDR F TH CVL RGHTS MVMNT

A big splash

Which way should the sea lion turn the bottom wheel so that the water pours into the tank? Each wheel turns in the opposite way to the one it touches.

On your bike

Which of the pictures below completes the pattern properly?

A

B

C

D

What a hoot

Can you rearrange the squares of this picture so they form a single night-time scene? Write the numbers associated with each square in the empty grid to show where each square should go. The first few have been done for you.

Egg hunt

These decorated eggs form a sequence. Can you complete the pattern on the last egg in each row with the correct number of spots?

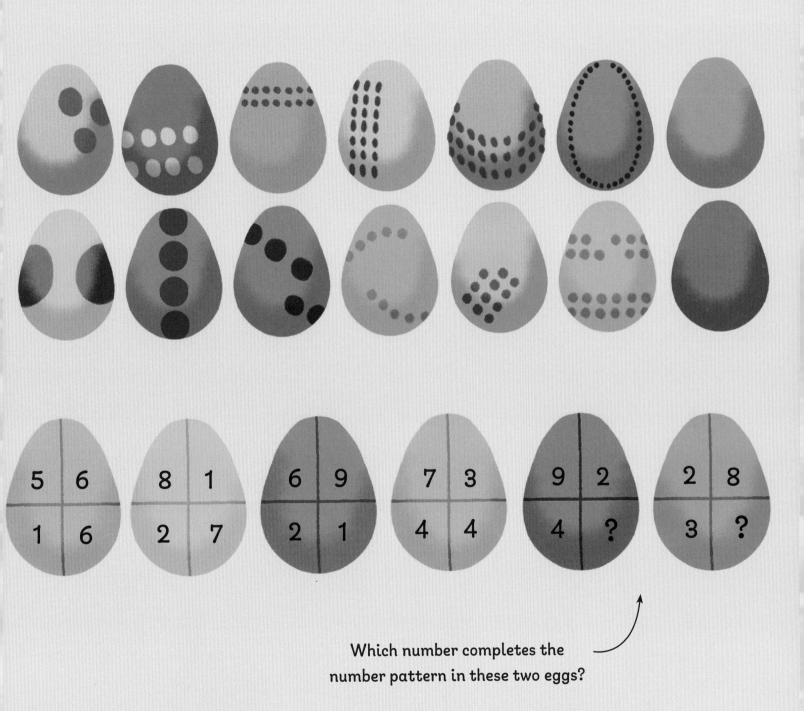

Which number completes the number pattern in these two eggs?

Here's a funny thing ...

Follow the instructions below the grid to find out the answer to the joke.

WHY CAN'T PENGUINS FLY?

BECAUSE	ONCE	OVER	WHENEVER	FLASH
CRASH	THEY	TOO	WISH	OUT
ROOM	HOPELESS	OF	CAN'T	RUSH
WITHOUT	WASH	AFFORD	SPLASH	BOOST
PLANE	OCEAN	DASH	AMAZING	SCHOOL
FALLING	FISH	COOL	FARES	OLD

Cross out any word with 7 or more letters.
Get rid of words containing OO.
Delete all the words that end in SH.
Lose any word that begins with O.

42

A smashing time

Which piñata is each birthday child having? Follow the trails to the piñatas to find out.

A bird's-eye view

What does this scene look like from above? Imagine you're soaring high in the sky, looking down on it, and decide which of the smaller scenes you would see.

A   B   C

D   E   F

Mind your step

The rain has left muddy puddles everywhere. Work out where is safe to step, and where isn't! Each cow has a muddy puddle in a square directly next to it. Use the clues to locate the others; one has been done for you.

A puddle can be above or below a cow, or to the side, but is never in a diagonal square.
A puddle is never next to another puddle, not even diagonally.
The grid numbers show how many puddles are in that row or column.

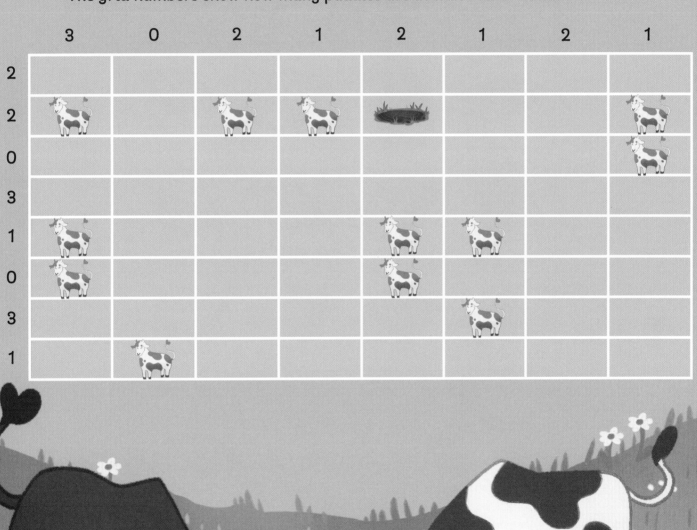

Page count

How many pages are in each type of book? The total for each row and column is shown on the right and at the bottom of the grid. Write the number of pages in the spaces below. All identical books have exactly the same number of pages as each other.

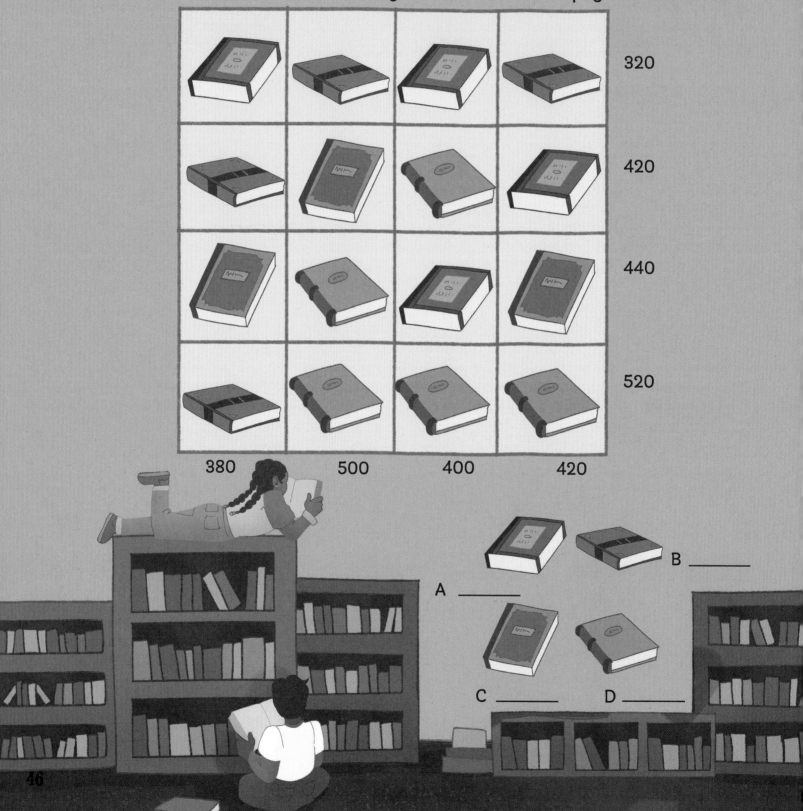

A _____

B _____

C _____

D _____

Llama drama

Can you spot ten differences between these two crazy scenes?

Fruit smoothies

Can you place the five different fruits below into the grid, one in each empty square, so that every horizontal row and vertical column contains five different fruits? To help you, some of the fruits are already in place.

Step back in time

Cross out every other letter to discover the name of four prehistoric reptiles. Can you match each one to the correct picture?

ZALSOMFOPSDAGUSRTUBS⃠QRUMEOTRZSABLFCROUAATWLQUHSUSSPTIYNHONSCAHUORPUDSTAINBKEYWLNOPSZAHUYRNUFSHEIL

DID YOU KNOW?
Although all of these creatures lived during the Cretaceous period, they weren't all dinosaurs. Some were classified as reptiles.

Hop along

Help the forest frog through the undergrowth so it can join its friend.

START

FINISH

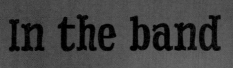

In the band

Take a look at this animal band at a rehearsal.
See if you can memorize where each band
member is playing, before turning the page.

In the band

Here they are on their first night! See if you can remember what has changed since the rehearsal on the previous page. Draw arrows to the place where each animal was playing before. Do not draw an arrow if the animal is in the same place as before.

Blockbusters

Jed, Ted, and Susie are having a movie night and have chosen one movie each to watch. Use the clues to cross out certain words, and see which three movie titles are left.

Cross out any word with 8 or more letters.

Get rid of any animals or creatures.

Delete any boy's or girl's names.

Lose any words beginning with P.

LION MATILDA DRAGON FANTASTIC WARS CASPER

INCREDIBLES ALICE STAR JAWS OF PAN NIGHTMARE

SPIDER THE DESPICABLE JULIET JURASSIC MUSIC

DOGS PETER SOUND WARDROBE PERCY RALPH ASSEMBLE

PIRATES CATS PARK HARRY BEAR POTTER GUARDIANS PEARL

CHARLOTTE

Art project

Maisie has photographed her Mother's Day bouquet and made it into a black and white picture. Which of these is Maisie's photo?

A

B

C

D

E

F

Dot to dot

This is a dot to dot with a difference! Join the dots to make a single continuous line looping through the grid. Not all the dots have to be joined, but each number must have the correct number of lines around it. Some lines have been put in place already.

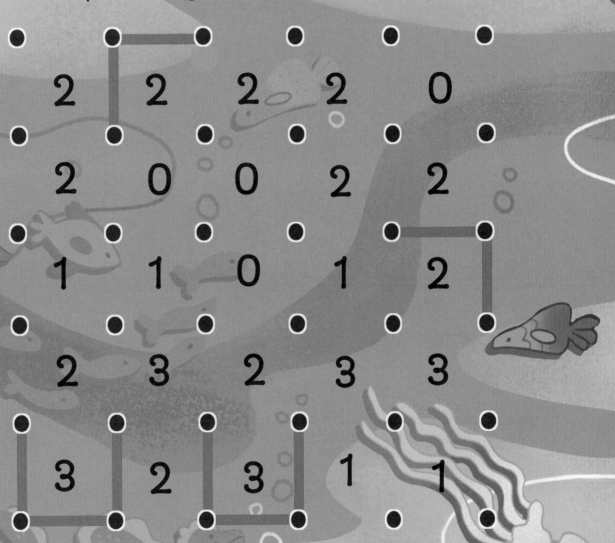

2 2 2 2 0

2 0 0 2 2

1 1 0 1 2

2 3 2 3 3

3 2 3 1 1

Sugar rush

One of these cupcakes does not belong with the rest.
Use the clues to figure out which cupcake should not be here!

It doesn't have a pink case.

It has sprinkles on top.

It has yellow frosting.

It isn't a chocolate cupcake.

Flight path

Help this witch find her way to a teen witch party. She has basic instructions but needs to navigate carefully.

Instructions:
If you reach a pine tree, head north.
If you reach a clock tower, head south.
If you reach a tree stump, head east.
If you reach a cemetery, head west.

START

Where is the party ... ?

Haunted house?

Observatory?

Posh hotel?

A head for heights

Look at the pyramid-shaped climbing frame below. Which of the views from above is an exact match?

A   B   C   D

Deep diving

Which of the kit boxes contains all the equipment that the diver needs?
The diver in the picture has all the equipment he needs.

Gone fishing

If you fold this flat shape into a cube, which of the six options does it make?

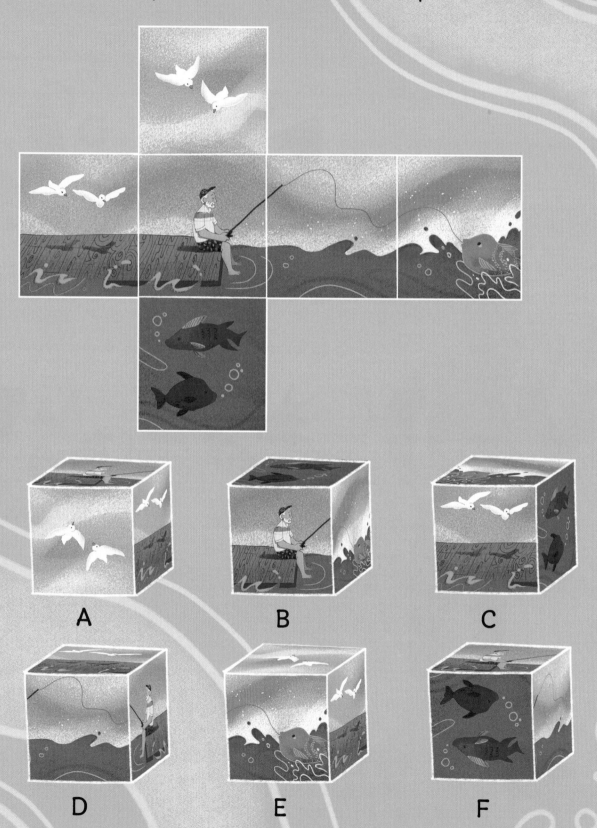

Fact finders

Figure out which of the groups of letters is the only one that can be rearranged to spell HIPPOPOTAMUS. Then find out some fascinating facts about these fabulous but fearsome creatures.

PPOPHIAMUPOS

SHIOMAPPOPMU

Hippos are the world's second largest land animal (after the elephant).

A male hippo can weigh as much as three small cars.

POTHIAMPOPUS

They can hold their breath underwater for up to five minutes.

HOMOPUSPPOTA

HAMUSIPPIPOT

They live to around 40 years old in the wild.

SHOPOTHIPAMU

Gotcha!

Draw a line through every donut, starting at X and finishing at Y. Your line cannot go diagonally. You can only visit a donut that is on a plate that matches the previous donut's frosting. For example, if you are on a pink donut, your next move must be to a pink plate.

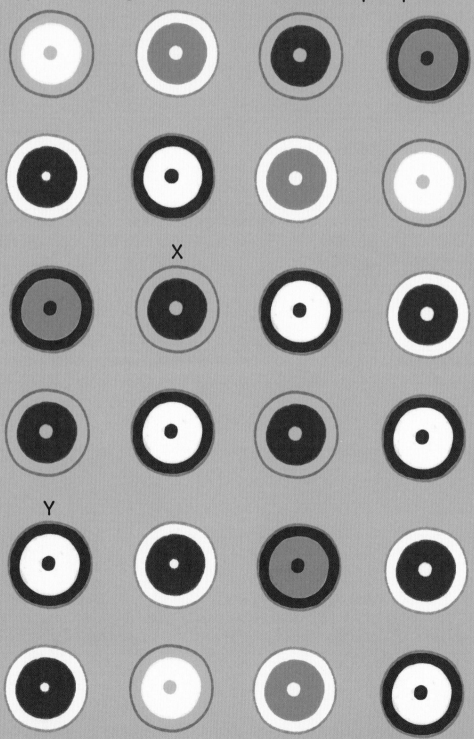

Cute chipmunk challenge

Can you use the following clues to work out which of the chipmunks is which?
Write their names in the spaces below.

Chester doesn't have a drink.

Chico isn't the smallest.

The largest isn't called Charlie.

Chico isn't wearing a hat.

_____   _____   _____

Dozy doe

Which of the bulldozers has completely cleared a path from the middle to the edge?

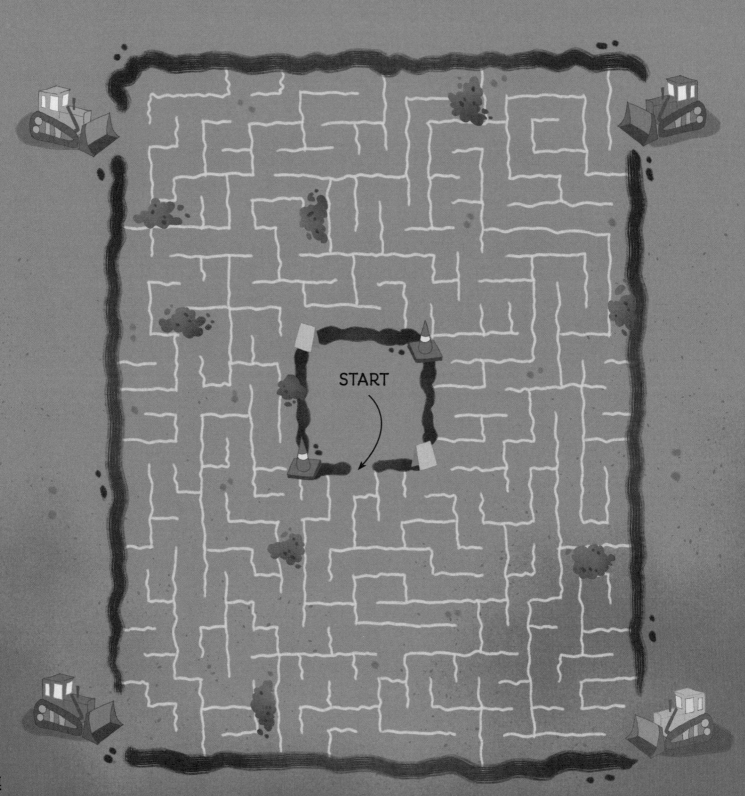

START

Space search

Can you find a tiny purple spiral galaxy, like this one, somewhere in the patch of space below?

Skeleton key

Maloney cannot remember which key opens the chest. Can you figure out which key fits? It's the one whose teeth fit neatly into the silhouette in the lock.

A

B

C

D

E

G

F

H

Best beak forward

Which of the birds doesn't quite match its reflection in the water?

Can you work out the name of these beautiful birds?

Move one letter forward in the alphabet each time. "A" is the next letter in the alphabet after "Z".

QNRDZSD RONNMAHKKR

Thirsty work

Solve the calculations on the dog bowls to work out which bowls have odd numbers on them. Use the letters on those bowls to spell one of the world's largest dog breeds.

M — 7 x 9
G — 128 – 46
R — 22 + 44
E — 96 ÷ 2
T — 19 + 21

D — 47 + 35
A — 121 ÷ 11
N — 202 – 6
S — 43 + 6
E — 64 ÷ 4

T — 17 x 3
H — 16 x 10
I — 72 ÷ 8
O — 2 x 565
U — 499 – 67

N — 4 x 96
F — 61 x 5
D — 72 ÷ 3
F — 112 – 19
R — 22 x 12

A tasty tour

Many states in the USA have a certain food that they are famous for. Work out each of these by crossing out any letter that appears twice on a plate and then rearranging the remaining letters.

_____ is famous for potatoes.

N A H
I D E Y E W
J W E J
Y O N

_____ is famous for maple syrup.

C E A O
V R M D T
V D N A C

_____ is famous for pecan pie.

O
H U X
U S T A C
C H E O

Y N M
G O G N
W Y
M A I

_____ is famous for corn.

R F L
L M R A
R O N
I E O F

_____ is famous for lobsters.

Hop to it

Which of the frogs in the corners will reach their friend on the lilypad? Each of them starts in their corner square. S3 means hop three squares south, and so on.

Frog A: E3, S3, E4, S4, W3, S2

Frog B: S5, W4, N3, W2, S6, W3, N4

Frog C: E6, N5, E2, N1, W6, S3

Frog D: N3, W5, N5, E3, S3, W6, N3

Hot spot

How many differences can you spot between these two scenes? Try to find all eight, if you can.

Take your pick

Which of the baked goodies is the baker making this morning? Start in the bottom right corner and follow the arrows by the number of squares marked, to see where you finish. Arrow 5 counts as your first move.

START
HERE

Nature trail

Help the butterfly flit from flower to flower to reach the big red flower at the end. The butterfly can't touch any frogs or birds, or cross its own path, and must travel in a single straight line between two flowers. It doesn't have to visit every flower.

START

FINISH

Space trip

Maria and her dad are on a tour of an amazing space site. Plot their route using the coordinates, and see what it reveals.

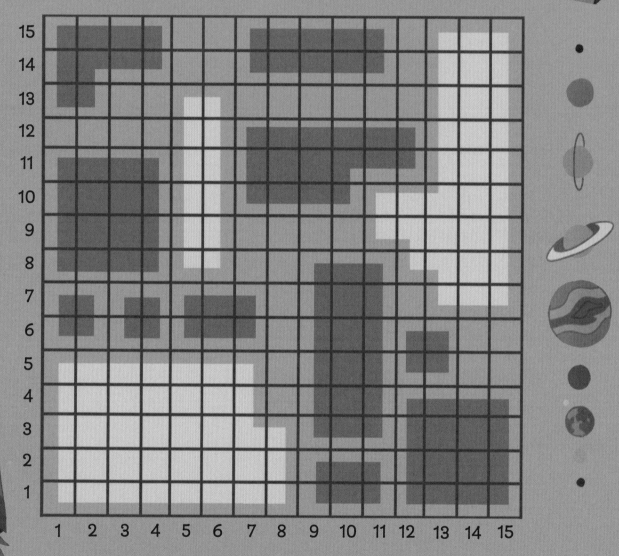

Join these coordinates; they are listed with horizontal first, then vertical.
(9,13) (8,15) (7,15) (6,13) (9,13) (9,8) (11,8) (11,2) (9,4) (8,4)
(8,8) (7,8) (7,4) (6,4) (4,2) (4,6) (6,8) (6,13)

Café culture

Life is hectic at the Drop In Café! See if you can find all five of the drinks, three times each.

Modern art

Can you find this detail somewhere in the grid? It actually appears three times, but has been rotated in some cases.

Get set, go

Can you rearrange the panels of this picture so they form a single racing car scene? Write the correct number order from left to right at the bottom.

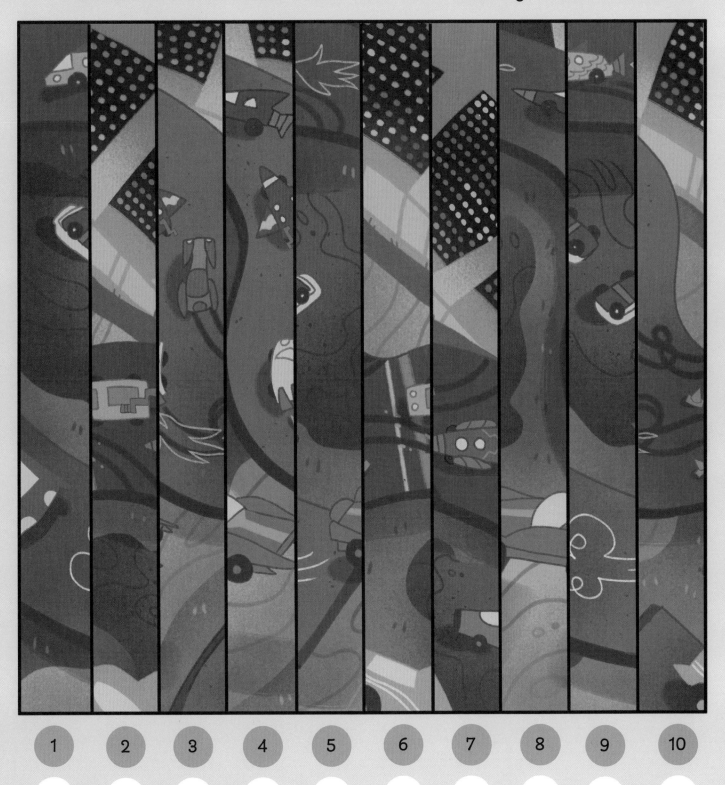

1 2 3 4 5 6 7 8 9 10

Crazy bugs

Draw a path to the bottom of the grid, from bug to bug, following them in the sequence shown to the right. You may travel left, right, up, and down but not diagonally.

A   B   C   D

START

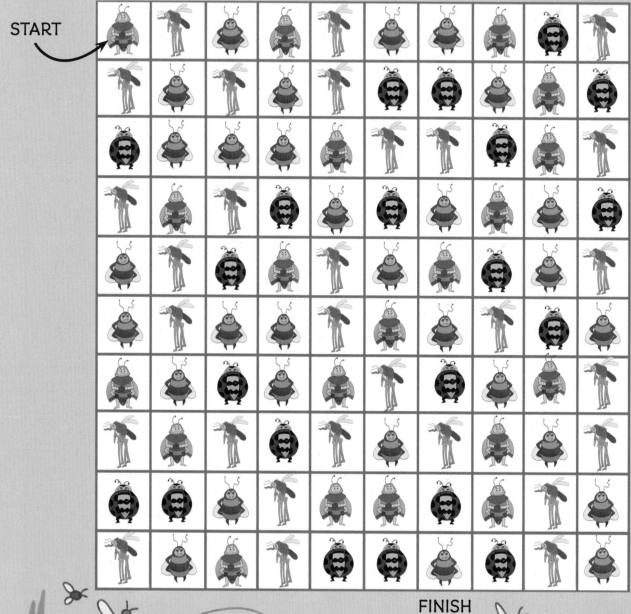

FINISH

Turtley brilliant

Can you work out what the pattern
is and then fill in the final turtle,
so it is sixth in the sequence?

Zoo trip

Which of these giraffes is the odd one out?

Which of these elephants is unlike the others?

Finally, which ostrich has a tiny difference?

Something missing

Work out which letter is missing from the whole puzzle, and then fill it in the blanks.

C _ N _ D _

M _ LT _

P _ N _ M _

P _ R _ GU _ Y

J _ M _ IC _

B _ RB _ DOS

M _ D _ G _ SC _ R

_ LB _ NI _

Busy as a ...

How many bees can you find in this image?

Pixel picture

Shade in the squares using the coordinates below to reveal a picture. The first number is the vertical squares, the second is the horizontal. Use a black pen for numbers in the black box and an orange pen for numbers in the orange box.

(8,3) (9,3) (10,3) (9,4) (10,4)
(11,4) (10,5) (11,5) (12,5) (7,6)
(8,6) (9,6) (10,6) (11,6) (12,6)
(13,6) (14,6) (6,7) (7,7) (8,7) (9,7)
(10,7) (11,7) (15,7) (3,8) (4,8)
(5,8) (6,8) (16,8) (3,9) (5,9) (13,9)
(16,9) (17,9) (3,10) (5,10) (16,10)
(17,10) (4,11) (5,11) (16,11) (17,11)
(3,12) (5,12) (16,12) (17,12) (3,13)
(5,13) (13,13) (16,13) (17,13) (3,14)
(4,14) (5,14) (6,14) (16,14) (6,15)
(7,15) (8,15) (9,15) (10,15) (11,15)
(15,15) (7,16) (8,16) (9,16) (10,16)
(11,16) (12,16) (13,16) (14,16)
(10,17) (11,17) (12,17) (9,18) (10,18)
(11,18) (12,18) (8,19) (9,19) (10,19)

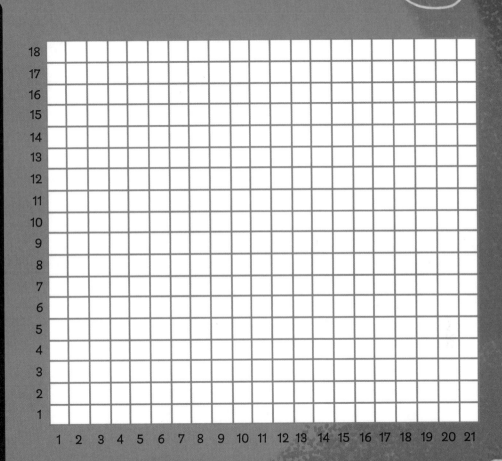

(4,9) (4,10) (11,10) (10,11) (11,11) (4,12) (11,12) (4,13)

Hungry Joe

Help Hungry Joe through the maze to collect each of the foods along the way. Which is the ONE food he won't pass on his way to the exit? You cannot retrace your path.

84

FINISH

Modern wonders

Some letters have been replaced by symbols. See if you can work out which symbol represents each letter, and what the list of words represents when it is complete. The same symbol stands for the same letter throughout this puzzle.

□H◆ GR◆᙭□ W᙭LL OF ✿HIN᙭

□᙭J M᙭H᙭L

□H◆ ✿OLOSS◆UM

M᙭✿HU PI✿✿HU

✿HRIS□ □H◆ R◆D◆◆M◆R

□H◆ ✿I□Y OF P◆□R᙭

✿HI✿H◆N I□Z᙭

Now you have completed the list, can you match each to the country where you can find it?

India

Mexico China

Jordan Brazil

Peru Italy

Baking day

Cross out any egg that has a number from the eight times table on it.
Use the remaining letters to spell the type of cake that the baker
is making today

O 44

C 18

I 56

V 64

T 42

A 24

R 19

H 56

I 32

R 82

O 48

L 40

T 72

A 36

It's all relative

Work out how old each member of the family is. Use a notebook for your working out space!

When my daughter was 15, I was 41. Now I'm twice her age.

I am six years younger than my brother. When my brother is 50, I will be twice my own current age. How old are we?

Fruit cube

Only one of these cubes can be made by folding up this pattern of squares.
Can you work out which one it is?

Ancient worship

The Ancient Egyptians had a variety of gods, and several of them sometimes took the form of an animal. Find the names of five of these animals hidden in these letters.

HCOWAJACKALTCATHFALCONOBABOONR

When you have found the animals, use the remaining letters (read from left to right) to spell the name of an important Egyptian goddess who was sometimes shown as a lioness.

Library trip

What book has Katie borrowed from the library? Follow the instructions to find out.

Cross out any word that begins and ends with the same letter.
Lose any word containing an A.
Delete all the words with a U in them.
Get rid of all the words with six letters or more.

OLYMPIAN	LABYRINTH	STARS	THE	HUNGER
FAULT	CHAMBER	TWILIGHT	DEATHLY	LORD
GOLDEN	CURSE	OF	SECRETS	GAMES
MONSTERS	OUR	ECLIPSE	THE	PHOENIX
WICKED	CRYPTIC	COMPASS	RINGS	ACADEMY

ANSWERS

PAGE 4

	Jacob	Mimi	Abe	Bo
Sandcastle			✔	
Swim	✔			
Paddleboard		✔		
Sunbathe				✔
Family				✔
School	✔			
Scouts		✔		
Friends			✔	

PAGE 5

Which are there more of, buildings with orange lights or buildings with blue lights?
BUILDINGS WITH BLUE LIGHTS

How many buildings are taller than the rainbow building?
5

Where is the building with a domed roof?

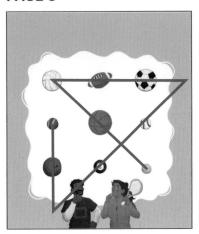

PAGE 6 It would take five moves. Move three limos from the left side and move two cars from the right side.

PAGE 7 ROCKHOPPER

PAGE 8

PAGE 9

PAGE 11

PAGE 15

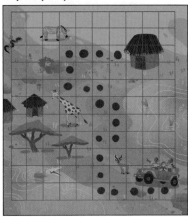

PAGE 10

1. 3
2. Parrot (macaw), eagle
3. Scarlet macaws
4. On the left, in the undergrowth
5. On the far left, by the snake
6. 3
7. The blue one
8. A peccary (wild pig)
9. 2
10. A spider monkey

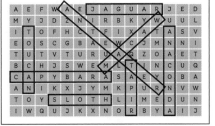

PAGE 12 1. PEGASUS, 2. SPHINX, 3. GRIFFIN.

Their common feature is wings; not all sphinxes have them, but Greek and Asian versions have the wings of an eagle.

PAGE 13 BRACELET, RING, NECKLACE, TIARA.

PAGE 14 Farmer Frieda lives on Hall Farm and has 2 ducklings. Farmer Tom lives on Blossom Farm and has 4 ducklings. Farmer Ben lives on Manor Farm and has 8 ducklings.

PAGE 16 W5, N3, E1, N2, W1, N1, W2, N2, E3

PAGE 17

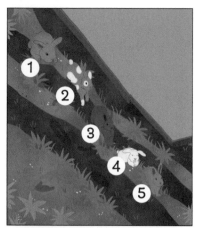

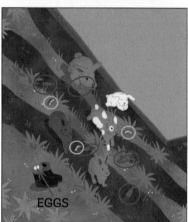

EGGS

Yes, there are enough carrots for each rabbit.

PAGE 18   CRAB, WHALE, SHARK, SQUID

PAGE 19

PAGE 20 There are only 12 pups so there are 8 missing.

PAGE 21 -

B – each row has one of each bottle shape, and one of each potion – red, purple, and green.

She uses four mixing jars for the green potion.

PAGE 22 -

PAGE 23 Here are some you might have thought of:
Cry, prey, same, spray, trap, pastry, pray, scary, star, come, meat, you, stare.

PAGE 24 -
1: D
2: A
3: J
4: F
5: K
6: H
7: C
8: G
9: I
10: B
11: L
12: E

PAGE 25 Serge played on the climbing frame on a rainy day. Caitlin played on the swings on a sunny day. Anna played on the slide on a windy day.

PAGE 26

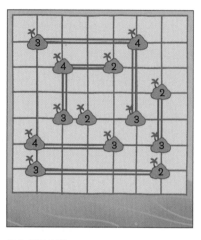

PAGE 27

PAGE 28

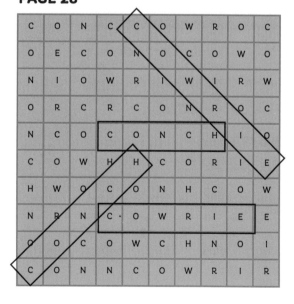

PAGE 29 No – there are 12 caterpillars, 24 butterflies, and only 30 flowers. 12 + 24 = 36

92

PAGE 30 -

PAGE 31 If there are 80 burgers, 12 get mushrooms, 20 can have onions, 32 get cheese, 44 receive pickle, and 60 of them can have tomato.

PAGE 32 Yes, she should arrive right on time!

PAGE 33 There are 18 prints.

We first set foot on the Moon in 1969.

PAGE 34

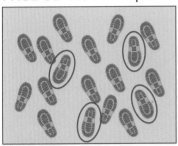

PAGE 35

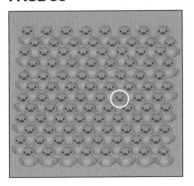

PAGE 36 SONORAN

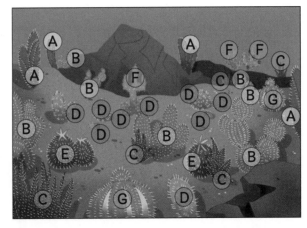

A 4
B 7
C 5
D 9
E 2
F 3
G 2

PAGE 37 VAKARDKR

Neil Armstrong FIRST MAN ON THE MOON
George Washington FIRST PRESIDENT OF THE UNITED STATES
Marie Curie FIRST FEMALE WINNER OF THE NOBEL PRIZE
Steve Jobs CO-FOUNDER OF THE APPLE COMPANY
Albert Einstein DEVELOPED THE THEORY OF RELATIVITY
Leonardo da Vinci PAINTED THE MONA LISA
Serena Williams ONE OF THE GREATEST TENNIS PLAYERS
Dwayne Johnson GREAT ACTOR KNOWN AS THE ROCK
Jane Austen GREAT ENGLISH NOVELIST
Martin Luther King LEADER OF THE CIVIL RIGHTS MOVEMENT

PAGE 38 It should turn it clockwise.

PAGE 39 C

PAGE 40

13	8	11	7
4	3	14	15
9	1	10	12
6	2	5	16

PAGE 41
Row 1: 3, 8, 14, 21, 29, 38, **48**
(+5, +6, +7, +8, +9, +10)
Row 2: 2, 4, 5, 10, 11, 22, **23**
(x2, +1, x2, +1, x2, +1)

3, 5 (each egg totals 18)

PAGE 42 THEY CAN'T AFFORD PLANE FARES.

PAGE 43

A = 4
B = 2
C = 1
D = 3

PAGE 44 E

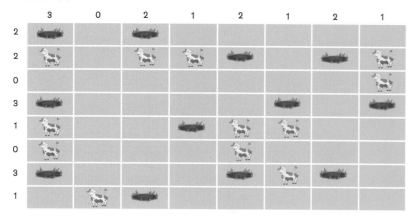

PAGE 45

PAGE 46
A = 60
B = 100
C = 120
D = 140

PAGE 47
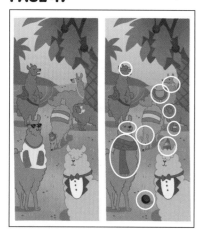

PAGE 48

PAGE 49
QUETZALCOATLUS →
SPINOSAURUS →
ANKYLOSAURUS →
ELASMOSAURUS →

PAGE 50

PAGES 51 & 52

PAGE 53 THE SOUND OF MUSIC, JAWS, STAR WARS

PAGE 54 B

PAGE 55

PAGE 56 B

PAGE 57 It is at the posh hotel.

PAGE 58 C

PAGE 59 D

PAGE 60 E

PAGE 61 POTHIAMPOPUS

PAGE 62
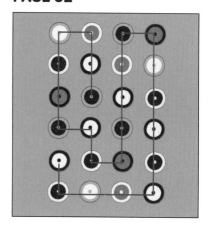

94

PAGE 63 Charlie Chipmunk has a drink and is the smallest.
Chico Chipmunk is wearing a coat and is on the right.
Chester Chipmunk has a hat and is the largest.

PAGE 64

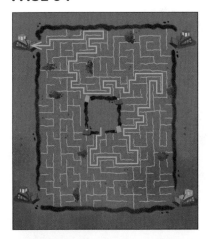

PAGE 65

PAGE 66 D

PAGE 67
Its full name is ROSEATE SPOONBILLS

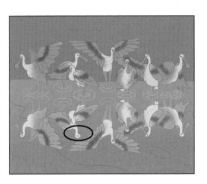

PAGE 68 MASTIFF

PAGE 69
IDAHO is famous for potatoes.
VERMONT is famous for maple syrup.
TEXAS is famous for pecan pie.
MAINE is famous for lobsters.
IOWA is famous for corn.

PAGE 70 C

PAGE 71

PAGE 72

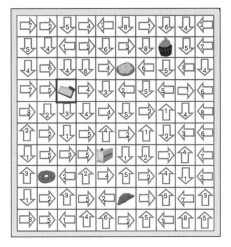

PAGE 73

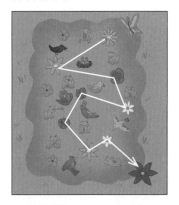

PAGE 74

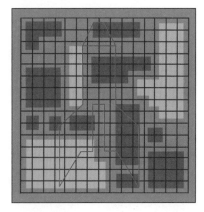

PAGE 75

PAGE 76

PAGE 77

1 9 5 8 4 3 10 6 2 7

PAGE 78

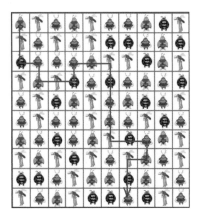

PAGE 79

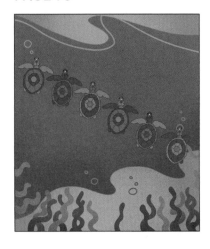

PAGE 80

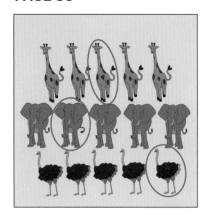

PAGE 81 They are all countries, with the letter A missing.

MALTA
CANADA
PANAMA
JAMAICA
PARAGUAY
BARBADOS
MADAGASCAR
ALBANIA

PAGE 82 -

PAGE 83

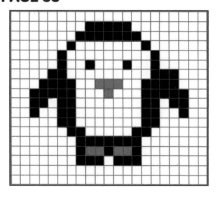

PAGE 84

PAGE 85 They are the seven modern wonders of the world:

THE GREAT WALL OF CHINA - China
TAJ MAHAL - India
THE COLOSSEUM - Italy
MACHU PICCHU - Peru
CHRIST THE REDEEMER - Brazil
THE CITY OF PETRA - Jordan
CHICHEN ITZA - Mexico

PAGE 86 7

PAGE 87 The mother is now 52.
The daughter is 26.
The sons are 28 and 22.

PAGE 88 C

PAGE 89 The animals are
COW, JACKAL, CAT, FALCON, BABOON.

The goddess's name is HATHOR.

PAGE 90 THE LORD OF THE RINGS